AF080368

This Sucks!
I Want to Live

Nick Spooner

Edited by Mona Gustafson Affinito

Wisdom Editions

Minneapolis

Minneapolis

FIRST EDITION NOVEMBER 2020
THIS SUCKS! Copyright © 2020 by Mona Gustafson Affinito.
All rights reserved.

No part of this book may be used or reproduced in any manner whatsoever without written permission except in the case of brief quotations used in critical articles and reviews. For information, write to Mona Gustafson Affnito, 723 Water Street, Suite 1001, Excelsior, MN 55331.

ISBN 978-1-950743-35-3

Printed in the United States of America.
10 9 8 7 6 5 4 3 2 1

Cover and interior design: Gary Lindberg

Nick Spooner, 1958–2019

"I am hoping that the ripple effect of my body 'dropping into the water' like a rock that ripples and ripples and ripples further outward keeps touching people well after I am gone."

This Sucks!
I Want to Live

Editor's Preface

Had life situations been different you would be recognizing this author's name for his published writings. But now you will know him for the person he created out of years of turmoil, struggle, pain, grit, and sensitivity—a person taken much too early, two months before his sixty-first birthday.

    I remember his telling of the appreciation and surprise when a teacher commended him on his writing talent and urged him to develop it. I remember pressing him to write, providing him with information about contests he might enter. Sandy Neal from Wampach's restaurant recalled his joy when he afforded a computer on which he might compose. But Nick had very little leisure for writing, busy instead living from day to day on earnings from his limousine business, keeping it in repair with parts from other vehicles. Then too there were the cats he rescued, cared for, and loved, and the occasional relaxing joy of sitting by the waters near his home, spotting the birds and the beauty of the clouds.

There were the nights he spent with his limo parked outside Wampach's restaurant, or at Turtles Bar and Grill, Pullman's Club or Babe's, waiting for customers to call for rides. They were his family – the whole city of Shakopee, it seems. "I remember him," people recalled when I went there to interview those who had known him. "A good man, generous, always willing to help." Sometimes he was at Babe's not waiting for customers to call but enjoying using his pretty good voice at Karaoke.

Nick was born on May 2, 1958. He died on March 23, 2019, managing to make it to one important date but not to his hoped-for goal. "God damn it, I am going to make it to the forty-two-year Medallion mark on March 13th!" he said, and he did, but he didn't make it to the farther goal. "Hell, I want to make it to the fiftieth-year Medallion mark because there are not too many people that've ever received a fifty-year medallion, so I want to be one of the only ones!"

Nick came into my life in spring, 2015 after I had rolled and totaled my Acura. Becoming neurotic about driving and crunching the auto expense numbers, I had decided to become car-free. As if the Cosmos were working its power, a friend provided me with Nick's business card. From the beginning he was "my driver," as long as I made my plans mostly for after 11:00 a.m. and reserved him ahead of time. After all, he worked all night, so he needed sleep time. I wasn't the only person who claimed him as "my driver."

I'd pop into the front seat and the conversation would start – from politics to Dr. Pimple Popper and everything in between: his excited pointing to a bird in flight (too fast and distant for me to see); or a lovely sunset. Sometimes we played with finding figures in the clouds. There were tales of his beloved rescued cats, or his latest project to improve the state of his limo or his living quarters. There was even advice to ditch the kitchen sponge –running it through the dish washer won't get the germs out. Or maybe it was meaningful appreciations of Tao or Jung, philosophic/psychological theories stimulated often by my opening comments as I popped into the passenger seat. Stories of his life – motorcycles flying off the road, struggles with addiction. His near death in his teen years when he was barely rescued struggling to make his way to the group home in an unanticipated snowstorm. The time he spent in "the system" and his release into an uneasy world at the age of eighteen.

Often, we dawdled in the driveway for more conversation. And always laughs. I was happy when Sandy Neal recognized my name, telling me Nick said our meetings always resulted in laughter. I didn't know his extreme scoliosis until the time he pulled up in front of the Chanhassen Dinner Theater and said, "Wait here. I'll open the door for you. They'll think you're someone important." Then I saw him standing and understood the back pain he sometimes casually mentioned.

On February 6, 2019, he drove me in a developing severe snowstorm to my dentist in the early afternoon. On our return, we sat in the car for a while as he told me his concerns that people might choose to walk home in the freezing cold weather. He had called his referral contacts telling them to keep customers safe inside. "Call me," he had said, "Don't let anyone walk home. I'll come and get them. It doesn't matter if they can pay me." That was Nick, and that was our last conversation.

He worked as usual on the night of February 6-7, sleeping some in the parking lot at Wampach's, waiting for calls from clients or perhaps outside Babe's (his Karaoke place). On one of his calls he helped a young woman home and waited until her difficult lock finally opened her door. That was Nick. He would make sure she was safe inside. As he left there, he called in a report to the police that he had spotted a car pulled off to the side of the road and waited there until he was sure officers had been dispatched. A short time later that same car, back on the road, spotted Nick's limo in a snowbank on the side of the road and called it in.

Nick had suffered a seizure, grateful later that he didn't have a customer in the car to suffer the witnessing of it. At the hospital he was eventually diagnosed with a glioblastoma – maybe more than one. Senators Ted Kennedy and John McCain died a year after their diagnosis, as did my former husband, Lou Affinito. Nick didn't even have a year. He died at 1:18 a.m. on March 23, 2019. Quietly, it was reported, but until those moments, he hadn't "Gone Gentle into that Good Night."

I received the news as I was attending a "One Day University" class on resilience- why some people overcome adversity and others do not. Nick had overcome so much with such grace. **Resilience**.

During our years of friendship, I pleaded with him to write. In fact, I have a folder marked "Nick's writings." In his last days, he had regular entries on Facebook which I have extracted. Someone should know the story of his last struggles and victories. In his final entry on March 21 he complained of falling. Just the day before he had asked, "Who would like to go to Lowe's or Home Depot with me? I need to find a polycarbonite tool case for a project that I'm working on." **Resilience**.

This little book is a tribute to the wonderful bright, caring, sensitive and interesting man he created. The writing is his, edited only for obvious typos and punctuation errors. I've included the Facebook entries on the dates and in the order he wrote them with occasional comments by the people who were there with him.

This is Nick Spooner's book. He is the author. His sister and others have more to tell after we first listen to him.

Mona Gustafson Affinito
Editor

A Sister's Tribute

I keep my big brother's photo by my bedside. I love him and I miss him. Nick took the best of so much suffering to grow into the wonderful, loving, kind, creative, smart, nature-loving person he was. No bird escaped his noticing and no homeless cat escaped his rescue. As he had rescued himself, he saved them. As he had struggled to find his own identity, he understood other's personal battles.

He's gone much too soon, but I hope this collection of things he wrote as he fought off his last illness will be appreciated by many as a loving memorial to him.

Cassandra Thurman

Nick on Facebook

Last entry before the seizure and diagnosis: February 6–7

Headache... backache. Can't take much more. I'm cracking. Don't go out if you don't have to. Seriously! The roads are deteriorating minute by minute, and since we are approaching blizzard range in terms of the Winds this afternoon I may not be out very long but we shall see later. If you're going to need anything from the stores I would highly recommend you get it now and then just hunker down until this passes tomorrow. So, just stay home and take a day off! I am going to try and stay on the road tonight for as long as I can but I'm not going to put a time limit on it at least not yet. If you really need a ride it's going to cost you!

> *Nick had been diagnosed with one, maybe two, glioblastomas on February 7. "They gave me two months to two years," he told me.*

Four days after the diagnosis: February 10

I need a ride home today...asap. Can anybody come and pick me up from HCMC and take me home?

Ok...now, I need a ride back to HCMC EARLY WEDNESDAY MORNING BY 5 AM for the biopsy.

February 11

I can't help it. I'm terrified. Brain cancer is never good.

Denise Nietupski for Nick Spooner: February 13:

> *It has been a very long day for Nick. He came out of surgery and is now sleeping comfortably in his room. The next couple of days will tell when he gets to leave the hospital. Right now, however, he isn't able to talk or take your calls. Give him a day and I'm sure he will love to talk to all of you!!*

February 15

Ok... taoist thought process. it is said if you are not dead then why worry about it. If you are dying worry about it then. So here's the deal. I'm Not Dead. The honest truth is I am dying and, like I said earlier, my timeline has been shortened. I may have two months or I may have two years. It is indeterminate. At this time I am living minute for minute. However, the joke here is that none of us makes it out of this lifetime alive! So there! Don't forget that! I just get to check out sooner but again I'm not going to worry about it until that time comes and maybe I'll have a little bit of fun along the way.

I don't want this to be serious. I want people to feel free to share their feelings around me with me because I'm sure more than a few tears are going to be shed. I have a few of my own to shed because I was hoping that this old wreck of a body would last another 20 years. I mean I'm only 60 years old my God! So yeah, check out time's a little too soon

February 17

I have been sprung out of Hospital jail for the time being. I cannot drive, since my license has been suspended because I had a major seizure which put me into a snowbank which is not where anyone wants to be. Thankfully I had already dropped my passenger off in Marystown before this all happened so she was safe thank God, and did not have to witness my seizure. How frightening that would have been!

February 18

My phone number is 952-220-0409, I accept phone calls and text messages. And jokes! Don't forget the goddamn jokes!

February 18

Okay! First, I am horrendous at updating. I am also pretty bad at asking for help but that's kind of where I'm at and I have to accept that fact. What I need right now is somebody who is willing to really take some time and muscle to shovel my deck as much as possible including salts or sand and/or any other good solid non slick surface for my deck so I don't fall because I'm a little wobbly still, although my balance is getting better but I don't want to take the chance on a slip and fall. Obviously. Then, if that path could be extended all the way out to the parking lot, that would mean a path about 75 ft long, total and approximately 20 to 24 inches wide. I wish I could do it myself, but I can't. My deck is a standard wooden deck and all I have are plastic shovels that are buried in the snow somewhere, and I have random stuff standing in the yard along with propane tanks so that would have to be shoveled around, so it WILL be a bit of a job.

I would like the snow on the deck completely cleared off somehow if possible. I'm just hoping to make it as non-slip as possible. I do have a good mat on the step in front of my door which I want to leave there. PM me or call me if this is something you can help me with. And thank you so much even if you can't, if you pass the word around. I need to be able to safely get in and out of the house so that I can navigate my way to and from doctor appointments which are going to start coming Fast and Furious.

February 19

Okay I know everybody wants to know what's going on with me, how am I feeling etc, I get that and that's okay! I'm glad you want to know, because that makes me feel good and wanted and cared for. Prior to today I was saying that this is a hell of a ride! Well, I've kind of changed my tune a little bit because now it feels more akin to being strapped to the side of a rocket and being blazed off the side of this thing we call Earth and there are no controls and I've got a blazing a**h*** which is the rocket propellant! Lol!!! How's that for a pretty picture! LOL!! It suits me, I just hope it made you laugh, because that's what I want!!!

I want to go out in a blaze of glory and kicking and screaming maybe in Terror or maybe in just the sheer thrill of the ride!!! Here's the thing that most people don't get. I get to choose. Nobody else does until they get where I am.

People are afraid to talk about death. People are afraid of death. I have been afraid of death but then a couple years ago it occurred to me that what I was really afraid of was a painful death. I'm not really afraid of death I'm just afraid of facing a painful death. But something has happened in the last 2 weeks and I don't know if I have changed, or if my thinking has changed, or if I have somehow developed some certainty about what happens after my last breath. I just don't know. But I am not now, anymore, afraid of death itself. Oh hell, I am pissed off! I am one pissed-off mofo! Because I'm not ready to leave! I feel like I have not left my mark on this world the way I wanted to. I wanted to have more of an impact. I wanted to leave the world better than when I came in. I am hoping that the ripple effect of my body "dropping into the water" like a rock ripples and ripples and ripples further outward and keeps touching people well after I am gone, and I can only hope that's the case. I spoke earlier of Zen thinking, being that, if it's not happening right now, why worry about it? Worry about it when it's actually happening. Well, honestly, I'm not sure I'm a very good Taoist, at least not in practice. Because I have not had the Taoist spiritual support that monks enjoy. But some of the things I have learned is that acceptance of what is, is in and of itself an art form and one of the most difficult things for humans to achieve. Acceptance of what is. Simply that! Wishing something were something it is not is a pointless endeavor!

However, the FEELINGS are not pointless because we are human, and we do have permission to wish something was not the way it is. However, that brings you back to the art form of acceptance. The ultimate yin and yang of life. The circle. To be blunt you can say it the way just about anyone has ever heard it said, and this is very Taoist Zen thinking, so close your eyes and hold your hands out, ask two someones to put a wish (and you don't know what that wish is) in one hand and have the other somebody crap in your other hand and do it at the same time and see which one fills first. YOU HAVE to ACCEPT the result. You get the reality that is served to you. You can either accept it and deal with it or pretend it doesn't exist and you still have to deal with it. It all boils down to which reality do you want? The one full of wishful thinking in which you acquire nothing of YOUR heart's desire, just maybe someone else's, because you don't know whose wish is going to land in your hand, will it be your wish, or someone else's wish? Or, just a pile of crap? Now hold on a second! This does not mean that you can't be upset with the reality that you are served, by all means if that is your reaction accept it and deal with it and be honest about it. Don't pretend you're happy with crap. However, if you have dealt yourself a load of crap, you have the option to make a different choice. Let go of the crap because there are way too many other options out there rather than hanging on to that one load of crap.

So when you go through the yin and yang reality of crap versus the reality of an empty wish it is very easy to be derailed by Simple human desire

February 19

All right, hold on, just a whole goddamn second! You know what I just read? I just read the titles of all kinds of articles and books on people or by people who have survived glioblastomas! Which means that even in spite of the "I'm not going down without a fight!" statements that I've been making, I gave up! What a dipstick I am! I didn't even do any research! Well now how silly is that?!

February 19

I have developed an affinity for Kodiak thermal socks!!!!! I love these things! They are so soft and comfortable and they're warm and, and, and, so if anybody feels so inclined, they have them at Walmart at $10 for a pack of three, which is insane! Go get some for yourself, you'll love them!

February 19

Okay, I'm really starting to get a better visual on the things that I'm going to need, to make my next several months or a year or maybe even couple years easy for me to dwell and live comfortably because, honestly, I don't want to move! I like my little sanctuary here because I look out my window and see woods and a creek and animals and birds and I need that because it is part of tapping into my Zen. Which I don't do enough of.

February 19

I have not owned a TV or a movie player of any kind for going on two decades, and I don't miss it. So I am not stir crazy in that respect. I don't need TV! I need books and I need my window to the wildlife!

February 19

This is my idea of an ideal living space. There Are Places out there that sell the Tuff Sheds which have porches on the front of them and they are roughly 10 x 20 ft and have a loft. And if I had had the space, and the land, I would have bought one of those sheds, tiny cabins, and plopped it up in the middle of the woods somewhere and I could live there dreamily for the rest of my life with a little bit of plumbing, a little bit of insulation and a propane heater and I would be as happy as any person could be! And I am not kidding! I would have little wild Critters roaming in and out of my little hovel, probably eating out of my hand, and birds would come and sit and chatter with me and tell me about their day and I could watch baby animals scamper and learn how to be animals and that would all be my Zen. Animals are the ultimate Zen.

February 19

Here's the deal, LOL! Okay, let me rephrase. Here's the deal, as I see it! And it's a different deal because just like in a card game every moment is different. you never know what's going to happen from one moment to the next so, as humans, we have a rather limited ability to see into the future like a crystal ball, so we don't know how to anticipate what the next moment might bring. And with Zen thinking, it relieves you of the stress of trying to guess. What this means is that Zen is the practice of TAO. (And TAO has a very unique pronunciation.) The T sound is heavily struck with a D sound, almost as if you are trying to push your tongue out of your mouth at the same time as you hit the T) and there is really no accurate English definition or translation of TAO. About the closest we can get is "The Way"

And Zen...hmm. how to describe Zen. Essentially, Zen is an act. Actually it's more an act of non-action consisting of action and thought. And the achievement of Zen is putting into practice the ACT of thought and of bringing oneself back to "Center" in which all that is and all that ever will be, exists all at that moment, in all of its possibilities. This endeavor is almost impossible for humans to achieve and it is because of the rattling that is constantly occurring in our brains. Passing judgement, theorizing, fantasizing, making up stories, creating fear and uncertainty and just plain making it tough to experience simply what is. our minds....our thinking, really is an endlessly running Infinity mechanism like the clacking Steel bearings that strike each other and cause the one on the opposite end to react and then clack back against the 1 it is next to which causes the other one to react and ad infinitum. That is the story of our brains and how they work. The art and the practice of Zen is to quiet that non-essential prattle in order that the observational part of the brain, what is also known as the lizard brain or your third eye which just watches, just observes, without judgment of any kind just observing. And achieving the serenity of observation allows the mind to absorb all that is at that one moment.

When you enter a state of acknowledgement of "what is" at that moment, and you are able to leave behind, as nonessential, what your own desires might be and are able to bring your focus fully to Bear upon ONLY what IS, right now, and nothing else. Not your expectations, not what you hoped it would be right now, not what you want it to be right now, nothing, expectation wise, at that point are you able to accept exactly what is, right now, and you have achieved TAO by way of Zen.

TAO is "the way", Zen is what happens when TAO is observed. Zen is acceptance, Zen is fulfillment and serenity because without expectation, we become fulfilled by everything because we have released our expectations and therefore are able to experience life as it REALLY is, not as we wish it would be or hope it could be. Which in human nature is as it should be and is usually not because we get caught up in the trappings of our expectations, and then our disappointments cause us to lose our connection to what is happening right now and our ability to absorb and experience it in all of its exquisite detail. It's kind of a strange dichotomy. Because on one hand TAO is you following the path, the way. You are seeking, you are searching for completement and purpose and meaning. And yet Zen is an act of acceptance of the flow of the way. And there is no right or wrong way. It simply is what is. Zen is "acceptance of"

Here then, is a simple exercise that will show you how easy and yet how difficult TAO and ZEN are. (there is a very good reason that the Asians love their gardens!) When you are wearing comfortable and loosely fitting clothing, find a peaceful place to sit, maybe in your backyard or in your bedroom, just somewhere free of human distraction. Sit. Close your eyes. Do nothing! breathe. Notice your breathing. Notice how it feels to inhale. Notice how it feels to exhale. Notice other things around you that you hear. Use lizard brain as "The Watcher," the one who notices and just watches with no expectation. Stay there and watch The Watcher. the Watcher is always aware. This is the only thing the Watcher does, is remain aware. The more you "become the Watcher," the closer to Zen you get. And the closer to complete love, fulfillment, purpose and meaning to life you get, because at that point you allow yourself to completely feel everything that is going on within and without your body and mind. And without that complete experience with no judgement, and no expectation, we are unfulfilled as human beings.

NOW, FEELINGS. This is a tough subject for anybody who happens to be a human being.

Feelings happen. Feelings are also TAO. Again, getting Zen with our emotions, and allowing The Watcher to watch and notice and experience without judgment or expectation is the goal of TAO. Because feelings truly are only feelings. They happen, and then they aren't happening anymore, just like breathing you take a breath and then you are not taking in a breath and then you exhale that breath and then you are not exhaling that breath, both a beginning and an ending. Everything begins and everything completes. TAO IS "The Way" Zen is acceptance OF it. Accept all that is, allow fears, worries, expectations, and judgement to slip away (they will), and you might notice a sudden upwelling of emotion. That is the opening of the love of heart and self and all that is. And you are within An Nth degree of Zen. Zen is about letting all go and accepting only what is, nothing more, nothing less. It is not impossible. However, it is extremely hard to allow our mind chatter to quiet.

February 20

Okay, this kind of sucks! Because I have been such a fiercely independent and self-reliant person since my teenhood years—oh, okay maybe just remove the word teen and leave the word "hood." LOL that probably would be a little more truthful. Cuz yeah, I was kind of a hoodlum. but it wasn't so much out of I just wanted to be mean and Reckless and a troublemaker. It was more out of I was searching for a reason to be. Because up until my twenties I had learned to believe that I had no reason to be alive and did not deserve to be alive and breathe anybody else's air. That I was wasted space. And it took me many years before I was able to start to accept myself as being a worthy person. And that I deserved anything, from anyone, including love, or respect, and these are still doubts that I struggle with every day, not as much as I used to, thankfully. But there is always the question in the back of my head, do I really? Am I really? And even if I believe it, does anybody else? and then suddenly, out of the blue seemingly, somebody calls me out on it, and I am confronted with "Nick, you inspire me!" And I get so rattled! Because of those questions, those doubts, (and they're the same doubts that everyone struggles with) because we don't trust ourselves because we don't believe in ourselves more than we believe in our doubts. This is a universal truth for all human beings. And this is why I speak of achieving Zen because it helps to remind me of my Humanity, and helps me own my doubts, and acknowledge my fears, and accept myself as being strong, and frail, and capable and courageous! And sometimes these are hard to accept about myself because I also have to fight the ongoing tape that plays in my head, the infinity machine that keeps replaying over and over and over how not worthy I am. Am I worthy enough to heal myself? Am I worthy enough to be healed? Do I deserve to live? And that one is the biggest question for me to look at and answer because so many times I struggled with, mind you, it was many, many decades ago when I struggled that sadly with should I take my own life or not, and thankfully I am not in that space anymore. This is why I am writing so much about TAO and ZEN. For me, drawing on Zen is a way to acknowledge my fears, my doubts, my belief system, and make sure that I am fully and completely present in the moment. Until you clear out the crap you cannot see the tools that you have or that you will need, so that is what I'm doing. And I'm trying to get into a fully acknowledged State of awareness. because to fight this battle I will need to be letting go, every day, of doubts and fears that might seize me, and be ready to release them the moment I notice they are there so that I can see the tools that I have on hand that will keep my strength up and my focus clear. God knows I need all the help on Focus that I can because apparently the swiss cheese in the old brain bucket, is becoming a little swissier and cheesier!!! Yes, there are more holes upstairs and so it's hard to navigate a mental straight line, let alone walk one! LOL and that's what sucks about all this because I really despise asking for help. I have to deal with my doubts about my capabilities. My belief system that if you ask for help you are weak. So I'm trying to clear that belief system so that I can move different beliefs into place, meaning a different tool kit! So, every time I state a personal need, it's a press. I'm pressing my own buttons and activating my own fears and doubts and what have you! And only by acknowledgement can I release those fears and doubts. Plus, when you move all the crap out of the way that's when you can start to have a little fun! Because then you're not tripping over the detritus that lays on the ground between you and your goal once you see what the goal is, which of course, you will not see if there's a bunch of garbage between you and the end goal!

February 20

If anybody finds out that they have random bottles of Diet Mountain Dew rolling around in their vehicle preferably unopened, and they just otherwise can't get rid of them, I will gladly take them off your hands if you felt like throwing them at my house if you happen to know where I live which is not hard. And my phone number is right up at the top of my page here. So feel free because other than the nasty water here and a couple of water bottles it's all I drink, basically. I will gladly throw a few coins at you cuz I know they're around $2 for a 2 L bottle

February 22

I'm tired and afraid to go to sleep. I want to wake up, dammit!!!

February 22

Okay, this is a little awkward, but I totally understand the situation of donation because I've had the same reluctance and questions about the people I am donating to actually receiving the money I donate. OR, Is it legitimate!!!! Because that's where I want my money to go. When I found out that somebody had set up a GoFundMe account for me, I wept. Because the last thing I ever thought was that I would need the kind of help that GoFundMe can do for people. Here's the deal. I know people get nervous about, and you hear all the stories about people taking advantage of GoFundMe. Hell, it makes ME reluctant to donate THROUGH "Go Fund me. But, and here is the awkwardness. I am not Wealthy by any stretch. Hell, sometimes I haven't been able to pay my bills. And my landlord where I live can be kind of difficult. But he's trying to run a business, so I understand, and I don't want to be the kind of person that lets him down, or anyone down. And when it comes to money struggles it's all too real for everybody! No, I am going to sign up for full disability via Social Security and, considering my diagnosis, that should be able to be fast-tracked. So, I should not need rent. But I will need help with propane to keep my house heated. Actually, I could use some furnace help as well but all in good time. KNOWing I have a bit of time left! (Not just assuming). To that end, I just want to let people know I have a personal PayPal account, which some of you know about because I have swiped your cards in order to pay for the rides and that has all gone right straight into my PayPal account and they have never ever messed with my money. And I have been with them for over a decade. So I have a long and good relationship with PayPal and they have helped me numerous times with the few different problems I've encountered with their program. So I would like to offer that up if people are uncomfortable with GoFundMe. My email address for Paypal is spnrnck @gmail.com and money transfers are actually quite easy. I've done them. So, as another option, that is available. And I can't thank everyone enough for the donations raised already! My God! That is Way Beyond anything I ever would have expected! Thank you so much thank you, thank you, thank you!

February 22

Okay, I have just been reduced to tears again. This time by my landlord who has always been a bit difficult to deal with because of the business he's trying to run and his awkwardness with people. And he just knocked on my door. And when I answered the door he asked me if I was okay because he had not seen my car's moving and then saw the side of my head where the surgery had been done for the biopsy and asked me, with so much concern in his eyes, was I okay? What's wrong? What happened? And when I told him I had put off calling him because it was going to be a hard call to make, I finally spit out what had happened and he physically staggered back a step and shook his head and said, "Oh my God I am so sorry Nick!" This man is so awkward around other people that he has his walls and defenses built up because, who knows why? And it doesn't matter, he'd come over to me and expressed his concern in a way he has never done before because, why should he? His concern is collecting rent and getting paid and keeping his business running. And that is as it should be. and just because he is awkward with people doesn't make him a bad person, but it does make him emotionally remote and hard to get to know. And this man took my hand, my shaking hand, and with one gentle squeeze conveyed so much compassion that I am simply reduced... and then he asked me if I needed to get out to see family. Where was my family? And when I told him that my little sister lives in Fredericksburg, West Virginia, he pulled out information on flights from his pocket. And I almost started bawling right there in front of him, as he told me don't wait and if you need to, we can bring her here and put her up for a week so that she can be with you. To say that I am floored is an understatement of epic proportions!

> *Nick's sister didn't make it while he was alive. "I was cooking dinner one night" she wrote. "I believe it was in February, and Nick called me. He was feeling uncertain about finding a doctor that would be willing to treat him. However, on that day he was ecstatic because he had finally found a doctor that said he would try. Nick was going in the next day for a consultation. He wanted to call and tell me about that and also his landlord had offered to pay for a ticket for me*

> *to go to Minnesota. I told him that I would come out in May so I could spend time with him on his birthday. He never once told me he wouldn't make it until May!*
>
> *I did go to Minnesota for his birthday in May, not to celebrate his birthday with him because he lost his fight on March 23, 2019, but to celebrate his life on his birthday at his favorite karaoke bar with family and friends. It was what he wanted, a gathering of family and friends remembering him!*

February 22

I have been on the phone for the last 45 minutes with Metro PCS who is my phone service provider, and have discovered that I am eligible for a phone upgrade which means possibly a new phone. And since this phone is probably a great boat anchor for one of those goofy little fish tank aerators that float up and down, I'm ready to get rid of this phone and go with something better because this one is dropping calls now or not opening applications up or all kinds of goofy weird things. So, if there is anybody who would be willing to drive me to a MetroPCS store, I would be so grateful. There is a store in the old MGM

Mall across from Dragon Cafe. However, they mostly speak Spanish, and considering I'm even having trouble processing English, because I'm just plain having trouble processing. I need somebody who can help me navigate through the whole process of getting a new phone. And finding out if I am eligible for a family plan with two lines, or whatever, but I also need to make sure I get the hotspot program as well so that if I need to I can pull out my tablet and get on the internet using my phone as a hotspot. So if there is anybody who is available in the next day or two, and is able or so willing to help me negotiate this process I would be very grateful because I need my phone for my upcoming hospital stays and or my continuing writing, etc. Thank you!!

February 22

Yay Rah LETS GO!! YAY RAH, LETS GO, NEVER GIVE UP, NEVER GO ALONE!!!!

MY BIGGEST GBM IS NOW NAMED HANIBAL FREEKIN LECTOR!!!!! If I'm gonna kill it, it's gotta have a name.....RIGHT?????!!!

February 23

Oh boy, I have one more thing on my bucket list that I have had on there for a long time and have completely forgotten about until right now. And that is that I have always wanted to be a motivational speaker. Not because I think I'm perfect. God only knows I'm far from it! But because I keep pushing through and I see other people stopping themselves just like I used to do! What I discovered so many years ago is that there is so much beauty in life.

We have the power to create a beautiful life out of the ashes of a burned and scorched life like mine started out. And with the help of so many others, which keeps me going today, I have been able to learn how to LIVE, and have a beautiful life! And I want to share all of my knowledge on how to create your own beautiful life, because it's not a secret, and it is not a mystery, and it is not something for only certain people! Everyone deserves a beautiful life rich with everything you ever thought you could dream of!!

GRATITUDE

> *"...with the help of so many others..."*
>
> *One person responding to the announcement of Nick's death offered the following on my blog:*
>
> *"I went to high school with Nick. I'm not sure how much he has told anyone about those days. Things were*

very rough in his life. Many years later, we ran into each other through an online computer bulletin board called Top City. We didn't know until a group of us met up for coffee, that we were old lost friends, as we went by handles rather than our names.

"We kept in touch from time to time after that, through more trials and tribulations. But, through it all, Nick smiled and persevered, always concerned about other people, and cats. We haven't talked in a couple of years, though. I was looking for him on Facebook to see if we could get together to catch up, when I saw the sad news.

"I am so glad he found so much happiness, finally, in his life. I'm only sorry it ended so soon. We are too young for this.

"While searching for information on Nick, I came across his note to the family of our high school principal. I will share the words here, as it was heartfelt, and I think it gives you a little bit of sense of his early days.

"To the DeLapp family,

"All of a sudden, I'm flooded with memories of Washburn upon reading about Mr. Delapps passing.

"I attended only one year (my senior) at Washburn, and unfortunately, I was one of his "handful" kids, minor trouble-maker, not following the rules, skirmishes with the law, etc. A handful. And, a troubled kid living in a group home. Suffice it to say that I spent quite a few hours in his office, explaining why I had done, or not done, any number of things.

"Looking back, and I hadn't until now, I can see that Mr. DeLapp must have stuck his neck out for me and believed in me. When I should have been kicked out of school, I wasn't. I was always given another chance. Because of Mr. DeLapp, and the teachers he hired, I found the strength to start believing in myself. The educators he hired had a huge amount of compassion for a lonely, scared kid, who was terribly behind on the credits I needed in order to graduate with my class. I was giv-

ing up, but they wouldn't, and that reflects mightily on the kind of man Mr. DeLapp was.

"It is said that a few words spoken with care by any one of us, can so deeply impact, that it can change a life. I just want you to know that the few words spoken by Mr. DeLapp actually spoke volumes to me! Of the few people in my life who've made the biggest impact, Mr. DeLapp was one of the last, and greatest gifts to me. He showed me it's ok to 'care' when I pretty much didn't anymore. He did absolutely change my life.

"I never got the chance to thank him. Thank you, Mr. DeLapp! Thank you so much!

"Nick Spooner"

It must have been a delight for Mr. DeLapp's family to receive this letter. What a reward for a good educator to know his or her work has made such a difference.

Thanks to Sheila A. Scott who shared this entry on my blog
Mona Gustafson Affinito

February 23

I have tried over the last several decades to live my life each day as if it were my last day. NO, it is not my last day!!! FAR ! FROM! IT! But as of this last month, everything has been brought into clear Focus that everything that I have learned about living everyday as if it were my last is being brought to bear, right now, as I speak. Because, it was all practice before. This is the real deal! This might be my last day, this might not be my last day. This could be YOUR last day! Because we don't know what each moment will bring us until we get there and that is the principal of TAO when you live each moment as if it's the only moment you have and you accept it (ZEN) and experience it fully, the next one doesn't matter until you get there and then you do the same thing, wash, rinse, repeat! LOL

February 23

Okay. I suspect that some of you are wondering about my symptomology. So here are some of the physical issues I'm dealing with. I have balance issues because one of the tumors has decided that I can no longer be a gymnast! I bet you didn't know I was a Nadia Comeniche in my secret life!!! Lol Yup, no more 4" balance beams for me! (Thank god!) But don't blame me if I fall over on the Dance Floor!

And no, even if it looks like it, I'm still not drinking alcohol! God damn it I am going to make it to The 42-year Medallion mark on March 13th! hell, I want to make it to The 50-year Medallion mark because there are not too many people that've ever received a 50-year medallion, so I want to be one of the only ones! Although I wish there were more people, I wish it was very common! But anyway, I digress. Another symptom I am struggling with is dizziness. And I know some of you will accuse me of having been a dizzy bastard for a long time anyway and that's all right lol.

February 23

More symptomology.....I shake. Lol. My right hand shakes like the dickens! It's weird watching it. It's like it's not a part of me. I've never had a tremor before so this is a first! Lol...now THAT was a funny....!!! ALL OF THIS IS A FIRST!!! Boy, I crack myself up!

February 23

Does anyone have one or two of those wall timers that you plug in your Christmas tree lights to for instance, where you pull out the little pin so you can set the timer for the lights to be on for however many hours and then they shut off automatically? I would really like to have two of those. One so that I can plug my crock pot in and because of my memory issues, it will shut my crockpot off after however many hours and I won't have to worry about burning the house down or destroying my Crock-Pot. Thank you in advance

February 23

I have a platform bed. And I have discovered that climbing into it can be quite the adventure. Right now I have a small stool and from there I step onto a metal folding chair which has its own treacherous adventures attached which so far I have not encountered, thank God! But I don't want to encounter them. So I'm wondering if there is somebody who can build a step that is approximately 24" tall that I can set the stool next to so that I can step from the stool onto the step and then climb onto the bed. I Envision the step being approximately 16" wide by 12" front to back and approximately 15 to 16" tall.

February 23

PLEASE DON'T EVEN LET YOUR FUR BABIES OUT WITHOUT BEING SECURELY TIED TO A LEAD ROPE!!! ANIMALS GET LOST AND DIE IN BLIZZARDS TOO !!!

February 23

Just about time to head outside, or take a nap ....
hmmmm

February 24

Okay here is the big writing for the night. I did the dishes! Yes, I did the dishes nothing more and nothing more simple than doing dishes and it felt very good to just do something so normal and it was so normal that it felt healing. So, I think I will dirty a few more so I can wash some more! Lol

February 24

I have just scared the liver out of myself because of the research I just did on how they apply the radiation to the brain tumors. On my best of days I do not deal with being restrained. I get over-anxious which can cause my fight or flight syndrome to be completely activated and I will go into a full, what is called an amygdala hijack where the amygdala floods the body. There are some warning signals that the life is at stake and in my case Panic ensues. Or I will go into full-blown rages that are uncontrollable and frightening to me even. And in the case of full brain radiation which is what I am looking at, it appears that there is a mesh mask that is fixed somehow to a table and your head is inserted into the mask and then the mask is cinched down to hold you tight so you cannot move. I am frightened, and I am trying to step into Zen, and it is not working!!! Because there is nothing I can do about it until I get there but my anxiety is already starting to ramp up. And I am hoping beyond hope that there is any other way that this can be done except that because that is out of my worst nightmare. Worse than any bug I can imagine including spiders. And I absolutely hate spiders. So, I am already terrified, and I just don't know what to do!!!!

February 24

So a neighbor last night took my 6qt. Crock-Pot, and threw in a huge roast along with potatoes and carrots and onions and God only knows what else! And then brought it back to my house so it could be plugged back in to finish cooking!!!OMG! Was that tops! Now tonight, I got a call from that same neighbor who would like to know would I like to have homemade split pea and ham soup? What? Are you freaking kidding me? That question should even be against the law!

February 24

My oldest kitty, Blue, is sticking very close to me the last week in a way she has never done before. She knows. I know she does, and she's confused but she is showing her love the only way kitties can do just snuggling up next to me and has been sleeping with me like she never did and she has been crawling into my lap like she's never done. She lets me touch her and hold her like I have never been able to do. So yes, she does know something's going on. And that makes me sad she's feeling a bit insecure. Poor baby. And Maggie keeps coming up and sticking her little nose right into my face and staring at me eye to eye, and then licking the back of my head from my neck up to right behind my right ear. As if she knows there is a wound there. Cats are such an incredibly perceptive animal. And I love them so much!

February 24

And another neighbor of mine works at a place that is like a bakery factory. And he dropped off a huge bag of oatmeal raisin cookies for me today! I am so blessed and it's not because of what's going on in my head!! About a month ago he dropped off a huge bag of cookies for me too before all this started. He found out I like cookies and there you go Nick! He also laughed uproariously, when he found out that he is now a cheerleader! On the Nick team!

February 24

My first chemo, radiation treatments are Wednesday 27th of February. I need to be there by 10 my appointment is at 10:45 but I don't want to mess this up even though I am so absolutely terrified I could pee my pants.

February 24

I. Am. Not. Brave. Enough! And I really need everybody to be there for me in thought or in heart or in spirit, on Wednesday morning as I tremble my way into the building for my first radiation treatment to find out what exactly, I am facing.... I have not been told what the procedure is for radiation. So I have no idea and I am a person who does not like not knowing. I do not like uncertainty that I have no control over. That is one of my worst nightmares worse than any Stephen King worse than any Peter Straub worse than any novel of horror and terror ever dreamt up. And I highly doubt they will allow anyone to sit in there with me and scream through my terror that I am okay and that I am not going to die in the next few minutes with a mask on my head. I'm afraid I will need a rubber room when this is all done.

February 24

I fell asleep last night, and there was a real comforting sound of two kittens chasing each other around and playing and for a while it almost felt like everything was normal. It almost made me believe that this is not happening. Then here come the tears again.

February 24

For the last 10 years since I moved into my camper in my little Sanctuary here in Chaska, I have been on call to go pick somebody up and take them where they need to go or I have been working on vehicles to make sure that when they call I can go and pick them up and take them where they need to go. That has been my life. And I live in my little camper backed up to a little spot of woods where I can watch animals and the creek rise and fall and I can listen to Nature and it's beautiful!

Now I can't do my work which, for me, is everything! Because it brings me out of myself and helps me connect to people in an easy way which for me is not always easy because I grew up with so many walls in place between me and everybody else, but I was able, through driving, first a taxi, and then my own transportation business, to build up some real friendships and relationships with so many people and I can't tell you in words how much I am missing you the last few weeks. I miss everybody so much! And I miss being able to be out muttering over, or kicking my car because I have to fix it again, or answering the phone and trying to figure out how to get everybody where they need to go all at the same time and only be one person able to do it. And now I can't work on my cars, I can't take your calls and figure out how to pick you up because my whole world is reduced to what I can reach around me. Everything I have in my hands has to go into a little tray in front of me or I forget where it is. This hurts so bad because I have always been able to rely on my brains to help me out of any tight Jam. And now I can't even rely on that. I feel destroyed as a human being, or, at least self-reliant human being.

February 24

My old laptop works as far as it will turn on and I can open files and such. So I have to teach myself that I can write "to it" (dear journal) and still have it be "to someone". But it's just not the same as jotting things down on Facebook so I'm struggling with that. I really want to write with you, the reader. Because I know so many of you who are reading my jottings. And it matters to me what you think, and it matters to me what you say. And writing to my other computer, well, it's just not the same. So, I have to somehow change my thinking, because writing on my other computer is about stories creating stories. Some are straight out of my imagination, others, well, they are personal experiences, so I have to get back into that headspace of sharing personal experiences on my other computer. Knowing, of course, I can always transfer files on to Facebook. And you, my loving and dearest readers, will still be able to share in my experiences as I share them with you. But considering the circumstances with which I write, and the fact that my brains still somehow ended up in the egg blender, I battle and I fight both with myself and my weakening grasp on the way I want to do it right, even though right now "right" is a foreign concept. Everything is twisted around and upside down much like a lemniscate (the infinity symbol) and I am left with no beginning or no end and nothing in the middle however it all ties back, now that I think about it, to TAO. The way. All that is, was, and ever will be which happens in all moments as we live. It also includes all possibilities, all options, all certainties, and all uncertain. So even though I feel lost, I am in fact exactly where I am. Which means I am not lost, I am here. and here is everywhere all at the same time and that feels pretty big.

February 24

I was just lamenting on the issues of trying to post to Facebook because I'm having problems with my phone and my hands don't work well, (well hello kitty) my post got lost and I am going to have to try and reconstruct it to some degree and it will, of course be different than what I had started out saying, and that becomes a frustration. The easiest things for me are becoming harder and harder to achieve. Just putting lines of peel and stick hooks on the wall so that I can hang all my keys, of which there are multitudes, so that I can label all the keys so that anybody can come in at the drop of a hat and grab a key off a hook and know exactly what it goes to. And something that would ever be easy for anybody including me, normally, is enough to almost put me on the floor. I am shaking like a leaf. And I had to go sit down. And now I have lost the post that I started to write. So,

February 24

You want to hear something really funny? I actually laughed out loud when I thought about this. I have been a smoker for 50 years. I do not own one real ashtray!

I quit smoking in my house about 6 or 7 years ago and got rid of all my ashtrays. And now, I am smoking in my house again. Because it doesn't matter to me anymore. However, there is this great freshener product called "Smoke Out" that really does cut the smell of smoke in an amazing way! I like the ashtrays that have the center tube that you can stuff the cigarette butt into which puts it out almost immediately. But also has the notch that you can stick a cigarette into which holds it securely over the ashtray. so if anybody knows where I can grab one like that whether at Walmart or wherever, please, let me know. Because the last thing I want to do is set down a cigarette........

Don't judge me for being a smoker, that is the least of my worries right now. I'm more concerned about not running out of propane to heat my place.

February 24

Between a friend of mine and I, we came up with a great idea that would help me with transporting my medical things including documents as well as keeping my personal desirable items close at hand and locked and safe in a transportable way. And that's hard to do sometimes but my friend came up with a great idea! So one part of the idea is, metal Camp cooler and it doesn't even have to be in perfect shape. However, it just has to be structurally sound so that I can mount it, or have it mounted onto a portable, foldable, luggage cart with two wheels. Then partitioned somehow so that I can put my laptop, my folder binder and one or two plano style partition trays which will contain pens and pencils and lighters and a harmonica and ipod. Just things that I need to keep at hand but if I set it down anywhere I will lose. And if it all goes into a cooler that locks with a padlock and is mounted to my luggage carrier and I can strap it to my wrist then I can use it also as a seat when my legs get wobbly. I'm thinking of approximately the 54 quart size and maybe metal would be too heavy so maybe it would have to be the plastic with Styrofoam filling with a metal brace inside and screws run through to metal straps on the outside with some kind of a hasp so that I can lock the whole thing and run a chain from it to my bed frame or wherever I might be unconscious or out -of-control of who's coming in or going out and what they might be taking. This combines transporting all my stuff including maybe you got a change of clothes and some snacks or drinks into a chair/bench so if my legs wobble I can sit down and I don't take the chance of falling again because my last two falls just recently bruised my tailbone quite a bit and I'm still struggling with that and it's very uncomfortable.

Who might be up for this little challenge?

February 24

ANYONE up for a short trek to my place to pick me up so that I can go to Babe's place for a little bit of karaoke tonight?

February 26

All right, I'm going to put this out and see what happens. I am struggling with a phone that really doesn't want to work well. Plus, I am also struggling with a computer that doesn't want to work very well either. It keeps cycling into "this PC did not start correctly so shut it down or restart," so I do that and then I power up, and then it says it didn't start up correctly so restart and then the whole process starts all over again into this whole cycle. So I need somebody who is a tech geek and not Greg Leske, who can get into my Toshiba netbook and figure out what the heck is going on with the startup procedures. It's a Toshiba Satellite netbook with Windows 10 on it Model # L15B1208X (something about startup partitions?)

And then I also have an iPod classic 30GB which has cracked glass on the front which I would like replaced if at all possible, and then completely erased or whatever you do with those things, and then loaded up with the kind of music that I like, blues and modern classical and meditation music and some rock music of certain artists, and the like...... so let me know if you have the talent for that or the time and how much it might cost me..... I really need to have that Netbook up and running because that will be my template for my writing that I need to get back to.

February 26

This is probably not going to mean a damn thing to anybody but me! But, of all of the books that are on my shelf in the cabinet, the very one that the kitten decides to pull out and topple to the floor, is The Celestine Prophecy. I think it's mysterious and amazing.

February 26

When you have done everything that scares you where do you go from there?

February 26

Oh, doggone it! I am going to have to teach myself how to type all over again! I don't remember. And with my eyes getting bad, and I was never a blind typer to begin with. I just became quick with the hunt and peck

February 26

Okay, I am going to put my neck out on the limb here and try something I have never ever done before. I am going to take an idea that I really wanted to do when I was very young and knew I should be doing when I grew up, and get on stage and be the singer I was always meant to be, up on stage, being the star of the show. I will need help to do that, obviously, but there are so many musicians and so many sound techy people in this town that I think it could be done in order for me to keep working, because I do have bills that need to be paid, meaning rent, electricity, buying propane for heat for my place, etc. If I can't drive anymore, then I have to figure out some other way to make money. Because I don't expect things for free. That's not how the world works. And, writing is a slow and ponderous procedure that takes a while to generate funds. So I figure if I could put together a show featuring moi, that with small donations at the door like a cover charge, I'd be able to start raising money so that I can pay people what needs to be paid.

YIKES! I just re-read what I just wrote, and I just scared the s*** out of myself! Like, what in the hell did you just say? And now I want to delete the whole damn thing like, I didn't write that!

February 26

Oh fer crine out loud! I just realized that if I go back to Wampach's one more meal that I will probably be welcomed OUT the door and told "Please don't come back unless you're just coming to sit and not eat." Because, it's a good possibility that everyone will probably think I'm trying to start a food fight because the Tremor in my right hand is getting bad enough that I'm starting to fling food everywhere! LOL

February 26

Well, it sounds like my appointments, daily, are going to be in the roughly, three-hour time range. My first appointment is with the medical oncologist dealing with the chemotherapy. And that is at 10:45 and then from there, and I don't know why it takes so long, but I go from there to the radiologist and my appointment at that is around 12:15 and takes about 1 hour, and yes, much to my dismay they will have to tranquilize me because my head does have to be held down via mask so that it does not move. And I have already spoken somewhat how about my PTSD panic disorder. So, I guess I find out what it's going to be like, tomorrow. And my heart is already starting to thump like mad!

I hope you all do realize that I am going to beat this s***! I got a whole bunch of years in front of me yet.

February 26

And once again, I am blown away by the kindness, the very simple kindness, of a man. My landlord informed me today that I never have to worry about moving. And not to worry about rent, or my past due electric, and that if I ever need a ride he is available. And we'll work it out somehow. I am reduced once again.

February 27

Maybe this hasn't been spotted yet, but I'm still wondering if there is anyone who might be able to take a small metal cooler or a lockbox or a strongbox even and affix it to the cart pictured here in such a way that it will hold binders, folders, a Plano style parts tray with the flip lid, and my laptop, and charge cords, etc. and also be affixed in such a way so that if my legs get tired I can use it as a little chair to sit on. I'm trying to create a locking "Go kit" that has everything I possibly might need for trips to the hospital or clinics or chemo or whatever. Or even just sitting in the house so that I know where everything is, because I forget so quickly where I have put something down. And I just don't want to have to try and think "What am I going to need to bring with me this time," it will always be in the case, locked up, and then I also don't have to worry about things being stolen at the hospital. So to that end, it has to be strong enough to park my 200lb ass on it when I sit on it, and yet not so big that it becomes hard to toss it in a car. So there are a number of considerations. It needs hasps, both to lock it to the cart, and to lock the box itself so the contents are okay. So I can put all of my valuables in the lock box with a combination lock on the box and key locks holding the box to the cart, and some kind of chain that I can use to chain the whole entire deal to my bed, or what have you, so that nobody walks away with it. So that way I can store my ID's and other valuables in the Box and everything will be contained and safe.

Is there anyone who is up for the challenge? I am going to be scrounging through Craigslist to see if there are any boxes out there cuz I don't want this to cost a ton of money! That is not the purpose of this!

February 27

Finally found my glasses, missing for two full days! So relieved!

February 28

How do you say goodbye to the people that you love and care for the most, even if it is a town that adopted you sort of ...

February 28

I have a small school bus that needs to be ransacked. It is full of junk and tools and odds and ends, because I have used it as a storage for so many years so I need people over the next month or two to come in and just take what they want. Not kidding. Most of it is just random crap. But maybe it has some value for someone. and the school bus itself can be taken if somebody is willing to put a battery and grab a 36 inch V belt and spend the time to try and get it running because it's been sitting for 11 years. They can have the bus for free. I will sign it over to them on the spot.

February 28

If anybody is available around 5 a.m. 5:30 a.m. and is willing to come and pick me up, I would love to go to Wampach's for breakfast this morning, If anyone is headed that way. But of course that would mean swinging out to the Chaska side of the river to pick me up. If that's something you think you'd be willing to do give me a call at 952 - 220 - 0 4 0 9 and thank you in advance very much!

February 28

Oh heck! I guess I'm going to have to give in and go on a journey to my most hated shopping Resort, Walmart! God, I hate that place!

March 1

Is there any chance somun be able to come grab me and run me to Babes tonight?

March 2

See ya'all tomorrow night at BABES! I'll be there with a song or two! Ok?

March 3

Well this kind of sucks! My propane tank just ran empty. And of course, it has to wait until 3 in the morning. I'm good until daylight so at least we're not fumbling about in the dark. And I do have a couple electric space heaters and I will stay awake in order to make sure that I am safe until somebody can come and switch over the propane line to a full tank which is going to be a messed up job in the best of situations and this is not the best of situations because it will require shoveling first. Not to mention finding out if I still have the two wrenches on the tanks in order to detach the line and run it to another tank. So I can only hope ... An additional note, I can do this down to 30 below zero so I am fine. I am in no danger of freezing even if the house becomes the same as the outdoor temperature. I am fine I have electricity, so I am good! And the temperature in the house is staying right at about 73 No it just went up to 75. So I'm good!!

March 4

What makes a person mortal? Is it your brain? Or is it the fact that a heart beats in your chest? This is one of the questions that is running through my brain as I ponder the tumors, or the resident aliens, as I think of them, that are also residing within the old brainpan. Hannibal Lecter, or the tumor that is on the right side is giving me some things to think about. But then there is Ed Gein who resides on the left who is also giving me some things to think about. All of them gruesome, but definitely worth a minute of time. Like I have said before, I have a very dark and twisted sense of humor. That includes having learned in the past about some very dark and twisted characters in The History of the United States, Hannibal Lecter of course not being one of them since he is an entirely made-up and fabricated movie character for audience titillation. Ed Gein, on the other hand, is an entirely too real character from Wisconsin near about smack-dab in the middle of the state and quite the character he was.

March 5

This may sound like a most arrogant question! But some of the comments I am hearing, in reference to me, myself, have left me puzzled and I'm amazed. Because I hear over and over again from different people who I'm thinking, in most cases don't know all the other people who are saying the same thing, and that is that, somehow, I am amazing. And I don't really understand where that word comes from in relation to me. And I'm hearing it from so many different directions that I am truly puzzled by it. And I just don't understand why so many seem to think that I am amazing, because I am just me. I am nobody special, and so I can't see anything that amazing about myself. So maybe it is time for me to ask you to tell me what you see about me that makes you think I am some amazing person, because otherwise, I don't get it! I really don't think I'm amazing, I am just like you. Every single one of you. Just a normal everyday person. I struggled with my fears about getting close to people and allowing them inside my heart, I have struggled with all kinds of different things so that makes me just like everybody else because we are always and all afraid, of something, and so we struggle. So that's why I asked because I think each and every one of you is amazing and have been amazing people in my life. Which maybe answers my own darn question, LOL!

Well doncha know! Hahhah!!! Lol

Oh yeah, Sandy Neal, keep your comments to yourself cuz I don't need any comments from the peanut gallery! LOL

March 6

CBD OIL is showing promise in the treatment of brain cancer. Who can talk to me about CBD OIL …

March 6

I really want to go to Babes tonight. I missed going last Sunday because I was too tired and ended up not arranging a ride to get there and then fell asleep. I finally found my list of songs that I had been looking for so there are a number of songs that I can pick from instead of the same old same old!!

March 6

UPDATE...FOUND ONE!!!

Is there anyone out there who has a small digital voice recorder that looks like the recorders of old, that took the mini cassette tapes? Mini cassette tapes won't work for me, but if you had a digital recorder or an SD card recorder where everything was stored on an SD card or something I would love to buy it from you, if you were willing to put it up for sale that is.

Let me know! I am almost desperate to find one! Or if you know of a store that sells them, like Best Buy, steer me in that direction. Walmart did not have any!

March 6

All right, so I am having a weird reaction, body-wise, that is strange. My skin feels almost as if I had gotten a sunburn and it is hypersensitive to everything! It's the strangest feeling.

March 6

Looks like I will be spending some time outside today! Supposed to be up over 20 degrees so that seems good to me!

March 6

I can't help it. I'm feeling a sense of Despair and sadness starting to creep over me...

March 7

I don't know of too many people who run the same hours I do. So here it is almost 3 in the morning and I am awake, as usual, and Restless, although not bored. I am never bored. I think I am incapable of being bored. There is just too much to do at any given moment. I could read, I could attempt to write, I could go and clean the toilet, or do dishes, or talk to my kitties, or roll up some cigarettes, or well, you get the picture. There are just too many things to do that being bored is just not in the picture! How can I be bored when there's always something to do if I wanted to do them. Or, even if I did not want to do them! LOL

March 8

Being independent, I miss being able to just jump in my car and go. I have an incredibly strong desire to start digging the snow out of the engine compartment and fire it up just to hear the motor running.

March 8

Benny X, I know you remember the ride to belle plain and back, Back in January. $50 each way. It's now March and you're still dogging me. Pay up man. Not cool. You said you'd drop it off at BABES if you couldn't catch me. How come I am still waiting?

March 8

Back in mid-January I asked somebody if he could work on my iPod because of the glass being cracked, and got no response until mid-February when I pestered him enough that he finally responded and told me he doesn't work on iPods well why didn't you tell me that back in mid-January? So, I still have an iPod 30 gig classic that still has cracked glass and I don't know how to delete all the email addresses that are on it, nor do I know how to load up music that I want on it so I need help with it. I would prefer to do the glass first, and not just throw a glass protector film on it because then I would worry about actually pulling the glass off if I were to ever pull the screen protector off for whatever reason. I would prefer to just have the regular glass replaced although I could probably tolerate just keeping it taped over or a screen protector on it. But then it's not perfect. I know, just me. But then I would like to find somebody who listens to like new age Jazz like

Chuck Mangione or darol anger William Ackerman, George Winston and other Windham Hill Artists and would be able to load music like that onto my iPod and I have an Amazon Echo Dot that I would be willing to trade for work done on the iPod....

March 8

Well, my first appt at St. Francis cancer center was Feb 27th and chemo hasn't even been started. Feeling like THEY just threw their hands up, shrugged, told me i had maybe a few months and to "take care of your affairs" and then they called it a day. Apparently, I don't have much of a medical "team". Guess I don't need cheerleaders.

March 8

I am going to see a Dr. Chen on March 29th, head of oncology at UofM hospitals. I'm done with St. Feancis.

March 9

I have a brand new Amazon Echo Dot for sale or trade! It's like the Alexa thing, just shorter. NIB.

March 9

I finally picked up some CBD oil. And took my first dose last night. At least now I'm doing something. And I'm feeling a little bit of relief from some of my anxiety.

Now, I just have to try to keep my anxiety levels down while I wait until March 29th which is the soonest that doctor Chen had an opening. But I am feeling incredibly behind the 8-ball and I'm afraid it's going to show and it's when I feel I have no control of a situation that I start getting a little snappy with people. So be prepared, if I ask you can I just vent? Because I am so angry about this diagnosis, and I'm so angry that Saint Francis hasn't done a damn thing yet, and I'm just plain angry! And I'm trying to stay positive, but it's becoming increasingly difficult! So, God damn it I may not be able to kick ass right now, but I am still taking names! This is A fucking Raw Deal, so you better believe I am pissed off! Fuck Zen! I'll catch up with that later! When I get there cuz I'm not there now, and frankly, I don't give a shit!

March 9

Okay. I am up against the wall. And I really need to load up my iPod and I can't use my phone for this because my phone is dying too. So with meditation type music to help me de-stress. Because stress and the bodily reaction that stress causes, I have discovered can make cancer treatment that much worse. And so I need to start meditation again -- something I haven't done in decades. And I really like meditation music which for me is considered New Age classical or New Age jazz Windham Hill artists, like George Winston, darol anger, Liz Story, Deuter.. William Ackerman. And so many more. The music they play helps me stay calm or become calmer and I find it really helps with my entire mindset in that when my stress levels are down, I can think clearer and process better. And since my seizure on February 8th, I'm having problems with stress and the seizure, which is a major short circuit in the brain as I'm sure many of you know. It did put some damage in my ability to process, which I am already seeing and because I see it it's a bit scary. So, having the ability to meditate by myself gives me the ability to see things from a new or different perspective. So, this is why it is so incredibly important to me to have my iPod fixed (the glass replaced) and then loaded up with music for meditation because I can zone out into that music and let my stresses go. Which, especially in this fight I am in right now, for my life, again, is going to be an incredibly big part of my Arsenal to bring to this fight. So if you can refer me to somebody who can fix my iPod for me, because my phone is in bad shape. Please refer me! Or have them call me, my phone number is at the top of this page right here. Thank you so much!!!!

March 9

Well, I made it out to one of the sheds in back and was able to double check on something, take care of something else that needed a weather check. And made it back into the house in one piece. Now I have another question. Is anybody ordering from Cub Foods for delivery? And then I saw here recently that Aldy's has some kind of delivery now, too. And my question is does anybody know how to set that up, and would you be able to help me do that because I want to go on a high alkaline diet, which means I need to switch over to a lot of fresh fruits and vegies. So I'm looking at potentially setting up for delivery because even on my best days I have always hated shopping oh, and of course now it's worse. So, having a delivery option available is wonderful except that my phone has gone from smartphone to the dumbest phone on the planet. And of course, my brain is not functioning, and I am not any kind of technical person when it comes to computer-Type stuff. I really need help so I can have food delivered to the house.

March 10

I am really hoping that there might be somebody who is up and willing to hop in the car and can come pick me up for a small grocery run. I know it's after midnight, but I'm a Night owl. I have cash (rolled coin) so am willing to throw some gas money into the deal. Just thinking Holiday. Not cub foods or like that. QUICK STOP ...not all night!

March 10

Kudos to Leah who I hope returns home safely because she braved the elements to come and get me out to the store and back home. Again, I am humbled and grateful. I pray that she makes it home safely.

March 10

I love my Shakopee family so much!!

March 10

I studied Transactional analysis (TA) once I heard about it and was able to use it to learn how to negotiate "emotional contracts" with people. Study it! It is very interesting! And it is also extremely helpful to those with social anxieties and PTSD like I have.

(Nick shared the following article on Facebook on March 10 because it reflects his beliefs.)

Higher Perspective

Jan. 29, 2016 05:34AM EST

16 of the most powerful quotes from Carl Jung

Carl Jung was among the deepest philosophical thinkers of the modern era. He examined many aspects of the self, trying to better understand the human experience.

Jung thought we were all spiritual beings, not simply a flesh and blood vessel experiencing the universe for no reason.

These are some of our favorite, most profound quotes of his...

"If you are a gifted person, it doesn't mean that you gained something. It means you have something to give back."

"One does not become enlightened by imagining figures of light but by making the darkness conscious."

"I am not what happened to me, I am what I choose to become."

"Until you make the unconscious conscious, it will direct your life and you will call it fate."

"Everything that irritates us about others can lead us to an understanding of ourselves."

"The meeting of two personalities is like the contact of two chemical substances: if there is any reaction, both are transformed."

"Knowing your own darkness is the best method for dealing with the darknesses of other people."

"Don't hold on to someone who's leaving, otherwise you won't meet the one who's coming."

"Your visions will become clear only when you can look into your own heart. Who looks outside, dreams; who looks inside, awakes."

"I am not what happened to me, I am what I choose to become."

"Mistakes are, after all, the foundations of truth, and if a man does not know what a thing is, it is at least an increase in knowledge if he knows what it is not."

"People will do anything, no matter how absurd, to avoid facing their own souls."

"Loneliness does not come from having no people around, but from being unable to communicate the things that seem important to oneself, or from holding certain views which others find inadmissible."

"Depression is like a woman in black. If she turns up, don't shoo her away. Invite her in, offer her a seat, treat her like a guest and listen to what she wants to say."

"A man who has not passed through the inferno of his passions has never overcome them."

> *"Your perception will become clear only when you can look into your soul."*

March 10

Apparently, pillowcases really don't make very good t-shirts somebody keeps stealing the sleeves!

March 10

My brother is a master electrician. I have been, ever since finding out about the diagnosis and that I had a seizure, none of which I actually remember but I have been seeking for answers as to how to kill these damn tumors! So of course being deprived of oxygen was one of the thoughts I had but of course that won't work because the rest of the brain also needs oxygen so I can't just pump the headspace full of nitrogen or something else although who knows what kind of trippiness that would be! Maybe it would be like being on the world's best mushrooms for all I know! LOL but then, I started thinking about the gamma rays for radiation and how they are impossible to completely target each and every tumor that I have since I apparently have quite a few. So that took me in a completely different direction, light Spectography, because in every science lab every cell can be broken down into what it's light spectrograph is, how it splits up a beam of light and every single cell has its own signature unless it's identical to another cell in which case then the light break up into the various colors would match up identical to each other. So that brought me to Royal Rife and the Spectography scope and his experiments with light spitting and cell growth. Which then made me think of something else. That everything has a specific frequency that it operates on including, inanimate objects.

For instance, think of the ability of somebody who can sing a perfect high C note can break glass because glass has a specific frequency and that is Hi-C and it will vibrate the molecules in the glass to the point where it will shatter! So I started thinking that if tumor cells we're able to be activated to the point where they self destruct using a small charge possibly even from a small battery pack, and that made me think of my brother, the master electrician. And then I started wondering, of course, LOL, could he handle looking at and dealing with a petri dish, or a slide full of tumor material out of my own head! LOL and be able to run electrical stimulation experiments on the cell matter of the tumors? And would he even want to? So, I placed a call to him and I'm waiting for him to call me back. Boy he has no clue what kind of question he's in for! This one probably is going to drop his jaw!!

March 11

Oh boy! I started tackling a very large very long needed project, today. And I am paying for it now and I'm not even done. But, my reward for doing it is, cookies! Yes! My neighbor buddy is going to bring over cookies and I am just so happy!

March 10 at 3:47 PM ·

Sorted clothes into keep (laundry) and "get rid of" piles ... finally. I have been meaning to do that since last spring! Talk about procrastination! LOL

March 11 at 3:43 PM

My balance has gotten so much worse. It's a little distressing. I can be walking forward and all of a sudden my gyroscope goes a little bonkers and next thing I know I am pitching off to the left and out of control. Makes me very glad that I live in a small camper trailer where I can pretty much touch every wall within a few inches so I don't have much space to stumble before I'm able to grab something so I don't land on the floor.

March 11 at 3:41 PM

I got a hold of Dr Chen's office today and found out that I will not have to call in every day to see if there is a cancellation. I am now on the list for a call back if somebody happens to cancel which is so awesome! So I don't even need to call in because they will call me how awesome is that?!

March 11 at 4:03 PM

All right, this is the sucky part that I really did not want to face but it's something I'm going to have to do or deal with penalties from the state. I have to go up to St Louis Park and stop and visit my insurance agent so I can voluntarily surrender my MNDOT. And tidy up that last loose end as I close down my business. Which I will have to do temporarily because of the medical restriction. So, is there anybody who is willing to drive me up to Glen Road which is right off of Highway 7 in St Louis Park not too far off Louisiana Avenue? It will probably take me no more than about half an hour to do. The ride up and back will take longer.

March 12 · 1:34 a.m.

Back in January, I asked a guy who does computer repair if he could work on my iPod because of the glass being cracked, and he said send me the model number, which I did. Then I got no response from him until mid-February when I pestered him enough that he finally responded and told me he doesn't work on iPods well why didn't you tell me that back in mid-January? So, I still have an iPod 30 gig classic that still has cracked glass and I don't know how to delete all the email addresses that are on it, nor do I know how to load up music that I want on it so I need help with it. I would prefer to do the glass first, and not just throw a glass protector film on it because then I would worry about actually pulling the glass off if I were to ever pull the screen protector off for whatever reason. I would prefer to just have the regular glass replaced although I could probably tolerate just keeping it taped over or a screen protector on it. But then it's not perfect. I know, just me. But then I would like to find somebody who listens to like new age Jazz like Chuck Mangione or darol anger William Ackerman, George Winston and other Windham Hill Artists and would be able to load music like that onto my iPod and I have an Amazon Echo Dot that I would be willing to trade for work done on the iPod.... Any possibilities?

March 12 at 6:47 AM

FSBO

**Gravel Gear (like carhart) hooded zipper jacket and bib overalls

**nylon, full zip legs/front, belted snowmobile suit

**sno- boots slip-on, zip inside ankle sz 13

**sno- boots full lace up sz 13(very nice)

All in very nice condition!!

$100 for all

Must sell

Please repost

Text/call

952-220-0409

March 12 · 6:49 a.m.

Brand NIB Amazon DOT

(Like Alexa)

Never been set up, never used. Make offer

March 12

I am not navigating this whole medical thing very well at all. I don't like doctors and hospitals even on my best day, it actually makes me extremely paranoid and trips my anxiety something fierce! And I end up with something like brain freeze when I have to deal with doctors because I avoid them like the plague because the first time I ever had anything serious to deal with medically was when I was about 15 years old and went through multiple back surgeries by myself. No support, no family, no nothing. And I was a ward of the state, considering I was incarcerated at St Cloud children's home at the time my scoliosis was discovered. So, I have been going to my daily appointments at Saint Francis Cancer "Care" Center and chit-chatting with the medical staff there instead of getting treatment, and I haven't known where to turn. So, I did take the bull by the horns a little bit, and I set up an appointment with a doctor at the University and now I'm also going to set up another appointment with an oncologist through the Methodist cancer system. And I guess I will see where that goes. I am not going to tolerate any more non treatment at Saint Francis. Please wish me luck because I have no faith in any medical establishment and never have. For example, I have set my own broken bones rather than go to a doctor to have it done. And I have also repaired gashes in my body rather than go get stitches because I would just as soon deal with my own pain then deal with a doctor and their bologna. And I'm feeling terribly beat down. I'm sorry to be so down in the mouth. I have tried so hard to maintain an upbeat attitude, but I kind of feel kicked to the curb.

March 13

Found money. Now I get to deal with found money. Found money is kind of a strange beast, because it's the kind of money you find in all these gift card bits. In other words the Speedy Rewards card from a long time ago that was reloadable and may still have a balance on it. So you have to call the phone number and entering the numbers on the card and find out if it's even still valid and then what kind of balance if any. And I have found cards with as much as six or seven dollars on it. And I found a Mills Fleet Farm card with almost $12 on it. I also have a Kansas City Steak Company gift card and there is $100 on it that I will never use now, and a $25 Outback Steakhouse card that I will also never use now, and if I don't find somebody who wants them then the money will go to waste. The money that, as cash I would gladly and gratefully use. So that is why found money is so tricky.

March 14 · 2:44 a.m.

Those who know me best will know that the word "can't" is not a word that is in my vocabulary nor is it something I say. I do not believe in that contraction. Why? Because as a child I had to endure being told all the time that I can't do things. And looking back I realize now, that it became a direct attack on my physical and mental abilities. So, in trying to prove that in fact I was able to do things, I found myself at the hand of trouble at all times, in that I was yelled at and beaten for doing things that I can't do. Only because I was trying to prove that not only could I do them (as in my abilities,) but that I could do them well! And as a child, of course that was me seeking approval, encouragement, support, fun and lovingness from the mother figure in my life. Instead she demeaned my very ableness. and then punished my abilities.

Can, not. Seriously, how can those two words even go together! You either can do something, or you are physically or mentally or, via time constraints, incapable of doing something. And if you say otherwise, then you are lying. Because if you say you can't do something that you are otherwise able to do then you are hedging the truth at the very least, or out-and-out lying at the most, when you say "I can't".

Tell the truth. You are unable to do something because....

Just admit it. Or, that you WON'T do something. Regardless. Just tell the truth! Be responsible for your choice. Telling a child that they can't do something is akin to telling them they are too stupid to do something.

Now, I know that not all people think or process incoming messages the same way. I am a good case in point. I take things extremely literally and personally. Always have, always will. And that is not something I have much control over based on my upbringing. So, one thing that I will never do with a child is tell them that they cannot do something. That they can't do something. I will always take the path of explaining that right now we need to do something else. And then you will show me what you can do, later. And I will promise them to observe whatever they want me to watch, and then I will encourage them to keep trying and keep attempting. Because at some point in their life they will need to be able to dig deep and find that Reserve within themselves to be able to keep going when it seems all hope is gone.

I try, every day, to plant that little seed of "I will figure out a way!" so that any young person (any PERSON) will somehow, some way succeed in life on their own Merit and on their own abilities....by showing them what determination looks like. From their own point of view. And how good it feels to achieve the goal, especially if they have to think outside the box in order to get there.

March 14 · 6:37 a.m.

So, I have this iPod that needs fixing. I also have a phone that needs to be replaced. The phone I was hoping I could somehow reset it and get it working right but apparently the battery has been cycled often enough that it is just not taking a charge anymore and not being able to hold a charge for very long. So since the battery is not replaceable this phone is pretty well done. Now, my thing is that if I have something that works, such as my iPod, why buy something else? My phone, on the other hand, is not working properly so I will be buying something else.

I thought about buying an MP3 player but then I am spending money to replace something that does work just needs a little help with the cracked glass. So the idea of spending money for something that would replace something else that I already own just irks me. I don't like it. I'm the kind of person that if I own a pair of tennis shoes, even if they are 10 years old and completely worn out, if they still work and they mostly cover my feet and they are still comfortable, I won't buy a new pair of tennis shoes because my old ones still work. Who cares if my toes are sticking out of them, they are MY toes, nobody else's, and I'm fine with it!

March 15

Great! One of my cats has decided that she likes CBD oil also (she licked the eyedropper when I wasn't looking) and now will try and grab it out of my hand when I'm dosing! LOL

March 15

It just occurred to me that I'm starting to feel like I am a pest, constantly asking people for rides. I'm sorry. The last thing I would ever want is for anybody to feel like they have to go out of their way for me.

March 16

Is anyone still out for a short time who'd be willing to come grab me for a Holiday run?

March 16 · 6:54 a.m.

On March 13th, a couple days ago, I accrued 15330 days of sobriety. In the translation that means 42 years. I still can't believe it! Because I really didn't think I would still be alive. And not only am I, but now I'm battling for my life again. Only this one I may not win even with my will do -can do, "one way or another" attitude. I may have to go into a hospice care center, and that scares the absolute fuck out of me! Because the kind of tumors I have are digging into my brain and who knows what kind of havoc they are going to cause as they dig deeper. Maybe, even though I take anti-seizure medication now, maybe they'll cause me to slip into unconsciousness and then into a coma and then my Independence and my self-determination will be taken out of my hands and I won't be able to decide for myself anymore. And that scares me and for those who know me well you probably have a pretty good idea of how private an individual I am and how intensely and fiercely protective of myself I am, and that I really don't trust that others will protect me ....

March 16 · 4:39 p.m.

Update because I'm dumb and didn't even consider that the ones who'd be best seeing this rant aren't going to.....for one reason or another (they aren't on here or whatever). So, i just wasted a lot of time practicing typing with one thumb. Ugh!!! So that was wasted time! Sorry folks!

THIS IS a compilation rant!!! Meaning, several incidents and comments over the last few weeks combined with one major pain I've been forced to deal with my entire life.

It has brought me to this fed-upness!!

What the hell is up with people telling ANYONE they should do this, they should do that and then getting pissy when the person doesn't "do that"? It's controlling and manipulative. And then getting pissed off when I don't do what they think I should do.

DON'T TELL people YOUR shoulds and shouldn'ts! And if you find yourself getting pissy with someone because they're not doing what you think they should do, then you better put a check on yourself!! Because maybe your "shoulds" are only an attempt to control others who don't want or NEED your control!

Travel your own damn path and quit worrying about the person next to you!

March 17

Wampach's REALLY sounds like a good idea to me right now!!! Anyone up for running over to grab me and taking me over to Wampach so I can have some breakfast and hang out with the crowd?

March 18

I have met so many great people since I started driving a taxi some ten years ago in the Shakopee area. And some of you encouraged me strongly, when I spoke of going out on my own as a town car driver. And you said you would stick with me through the transition if I should do that and become my own businessman. And you did stick with me. And through all these intervening years, you have stuck by my side through engine blow ups, and my own shortcomings. Where I have fallen short of my promises to take care of you and yet, for the most part, you have always forgiven me and given me another chance. You all are amazing. I can't say it enough and I can't thank you enough! By the way, you're still going to see me wobbling around. It's not like I'm turning into a shriveled-up old prune! I still have songs to sing and jokes, and I need your jokes as well cuz I'm running out, rapidly! So, help me out here! Who is not afraid to call me? My phone has gone silent. And so one by one I have been trying to call people and let them know I think about you and I want you to stay in my life and we don't have to talk about my tumors, as a matter of fact I have doctors I can talk to about them so you don't have to. I mean, for real? Who wants to sit and talk about somebody's tumors!?! ugh!!that would get old really quick! LOL! I would rather talk about falling into the mud pit that's my front yard! Lol now that was funny!

March 18

UPDATE 6:15 PM

Got a ride!!! Thank you!!!!

I am looking for a ride at 1 p.m. on Friday the 22nd this week, to take me up to the Frauenschuh clinic in St Louis Park off of Excelsior Boulevard and Louisiana Avenue for a follow-up appointment with my new oncologist who I happen to like very much! I don't know how long the appointment is going to take because I think it's going to include my first round of chemo and possibly my first round of radiation. So if you can do it, it might be awhile before I can be taken home. What I liked about him, is that he is in total accord with me about even if he can only extend my life by a matter of days, I have the right to not just want those days, but expect him to help me to fight for those days as well. And, he is on board about any cannabinoid assistance if necessary.

March 18 · 2:42p.m.

Starting chemo this weekend. I am nervous, because I know there's going to be nausea and I will probably get weak but one way or another it'll be fine. And radiation starts next week. That makes me even more nervous because of my PTSD and anxiety and the fact that they have to fit me with some kind of a mask for my head and that has to be somehow fastened to the table so that my head does not move at all while they are doing the radiation. but what worries me the most, is the spasms that will happen in my back because of my fusions. So, this Friday at my first appointment for review, I will be discussing with the doctor how we can mitigate muscle spasms before we even start. And because of my conversation with him last Friday, I know he will be able to work with me and my back issues. But I'm still nervous because of the trial and error part of it. I feel like I finally have some kind of medical backup that actually gives a fuck about me. Saint Francis? Who the hell are they? They took any sense of positivity right out of my heart. And now, for the first time in almost a month I feel like I have a bit of Hope. At least I got somebody who will fight with me! Saint Francis pulled the fight right out of me because they took it right out of my hands. Damn it I got my fight back!!! LETS GO!!!!

IT'S TIME TO ROCK AND ROLL!!!!!

March 18 · 4:23 p.m.

I REALLY need to get laundry done! Gotta make a plan here....

March 19 · at 6:36 a.m.

$25 caribou gift card, unused (full balance left) trade for? Have a $25 visa and a $50 visa (both gift cards non-reloadable) can be used anywhere accepts visa, (caribou only at caribou obviously) so in total, $100 trade for?

(MP3? player? Loaded with music of my choice) or buy them straight up, I will take cash too. It's easy to call for balance confirmation....

March 20

Who would like to go to Lowe's or Home Depot with me? I need to find a polycarbonate tool case for a project that I am working on

March 21 · 1:59 a.m.

Dammit all to hell!!!

What I was afraid might happen has happened! Dammit I am now in the category of fall risk.

I'm like the drunk person who goes down once and is never really able to completely regain their balance even after being stood up and steadied. Down they go again! Well, that is now me! Dammit!!!! I think what scares me the most other than the sudden pitching over, is the fact that I have no strength in my arms to really catch myself. They just collapse. I can pick myself up again, so that is not a problem, but if my arms give out in the process, down I go again. Dammit, dammit, damn it! This sucks

> ***THIS IS THE END OF NICK'S FACEBOOK ENTRIES.***

The Memorial

On January 25th, 2020 Nick's four siblings went to the Memorial Park in Shakopee, MN. to say Their final goodbyes.

"He loved nature," Cassandra said, "and he LOVED watching birds. The Minnesota river flows through the park and there is a beautiful area where ducks and swans swim that made this area particularly perfect."

This is the poem she wrote and read:

> *What moves through us is a silence,*
> *a quiet sadness,*
> *a longing for one more day,*
> *one more word,*
> *one more touch.*

We may not understand why you left this world so soon,

or why you left before we were ready to say good-bye,

but...little by little,

we begin to remember not that you died,

but that you lived.

And that your life gave us memories

too beautiful to ever forget.

"The day was sunny, around 34 degrees, with no wind. There was snow on the ground, so footing was a little bit unsteady. My bother Earl had to step down the embankment and hold on to a tree with one hand while spreading Nick's ashes into the flowing water with the other. Earl started laughing as he leaned out over the water and he said 'Nick would have loved this. He is most certainly looking down and laughing at us right now.'"

Final Memories of Big Brother Nick

Nick was born Pamela Kay Olson on May 2nd, 1958, the second child to Howard Dean Olson and Myra Madelyn Olson (Ramstad). Bonnie Jean was born in April the previous year, blind from crushed optical nerves due to an injury Myra sustained that caused her water to break and a dry birth to ensue. From my earliest memories I cannot remember a time when Nick was not by Bonnie's side. Not only was he asked to keep Bonnie company, but he was often asked to watch over me.

One of my favorite things when I was young was sitting between Bonnie and Nick at our piano while Bonnie played and they both sang. He had a pretty good voice!

As long as I can remember Nick hated wearing dresses. He would argue vehemently with our mom when she wanted him to dress up to go see our grandparents, or for a school event. I remember him always wearing jeans and long sleeve button up shirts

In his teens he had to have back surgery for his scoliosis and wear a back brace. He was miserable during this time. He felt slow and clumsy. This was when he went to live in a group home.

When I was twelve and Nick nineteen, he came to my school. With Mom's permission, he took me out of school so he could talk with me. He revealed he was a lesbian. I did not understand what that was but if Nick was doing it, it must be cool. He was wearing biker/hiking boots, a black leather jacket, blue t-shirt, and dark blue jeans. I found out later that day that he had bought a motorcycle.

When I was fifteen, I had to stay with Nick for two weeks because mom had lung cancer and had to go to hospital to have surgery. He was going by the name Marsh at that time. That is when I found out what it meant to be lesbian. It was confusing to see two girls kissing and I did not know what to think so I went home the next morning without telling Nick. He panicked because he did not know where I had gone but I called mom at the hospital and she told Nick later that day.

I did not speak with him for a couple of years, but I think he understood. He was always so patient once he was on his own. When he was younger, he would get so angry at times. I think his anger was mostly because he was confused about who he was and the times (the 70's) did not help because terminology for the LGBTQ community was not present in MN. Most people were closed minded homophobes then.

Persecution happened to anyone that was openly gay or lesbian. In fact, I remember Nick telling me about a time in MN when the courts were holding what he called "The Minnesota Witch Trials." He said they were bringing in people of color, gang members, LGBTQ members, as well as others. He was slated to appear in court 3 days after the trials ended. I cannot remember what he said the trials were about, but he said a few of his friends disappeared during this time and he never knew what happened to them. I believe this was in the late 1970's-very early 1980's.

It was not until he was living on his own and found the LGTBQ community that he was able to start expressing himself and exploring who he was. I don't know the exact time when he knew male was the right gender for him. I suspect he always knew but going against what society taught you from birth is a hard nut to crack.

Nick Spooner is the name he finally chose. Spooner is my Grandmother's maiden name on my mother's side. I think he always knew he was not female but when you grow up in a society that does not have terminology and is very against anything that is not "normal" you hide inside yourself.

One of the things I admired about Nick was his ability to face his fears head on. One fear he had was of small children. I suspect that fear came about when I was born. I know he was expected to help my mom with me and honestly in that day and age (girls) were expected to help with all household chores and younger children. I think he had anxiety when he had to take care of me because he felt not up to the task, afraid to do something wrong. So when I got married and started having children his relationship with me changed. The only time I saw him was at mom's house for Thanksgiving, Christmas, or Easter. We would talk occasionally on the phone but with his life, and me having 4 children, all of them about 2 years apart, we rarely found time to talk. There was one time when I was pregnant with my 3rd child, I had gone into labor at night and had no one to watch my 2 boys at the time. Not having a better solution, I called Nick up about 11pm and asked, practically begged him to come and sit with the boys so I could go to the hospital. To my astonishment he said he would do it! That was my Nick! Always willing to help regardless of the circumstances.

Cassandra Thurman

Epilogue from a Friend

I first met Pam Olson during 12th grade at Washburn High School in Minneapolis. After classes, we hung out on the front steps of the school smoking cigarettes, if we had them, and talking about starting an all chick biker gang. Another friend of ours would sit with us until her boyfriend who was in a biker gang would pull up on his bike and pick her up. Then we would wander our own separate directions.

She did not have many friends. Kind of a loner and taller than most of the kids. We all knew she was living at St Joe's home for kids, but I don't think we ever knew exactly how to deal with the kids who lived there.

She told me she had a rough life. I don't remember about her birth family, but after being at St. Joe's for a while she was placed at a woman's home, a foster home, in the Washburn District. So she got to continue at Washburn.

She missed a lot of school for Court reasons and part way through the school year she was out for medical reasons. She came back to school with a full body cast which made her look even larger and taller. People would stare and step out of her way in the hallways. We continued to be friends though we didn't hang out except for in front of the school right after class.

In the spring, her cast was off. She was in my civics class and told me she was going to Washington DC for the women's March. I was so jealous; I asked her how that could possibly happen since she had missed so much school already. She told me she had talked with the principal and all of her teachers and the agreement was that when she came back from Washington DC she would give a report to all the Civics classes starting with ours.

I knew her trip was being funded by the Minneapolis chapter of NOW. I thought that was so cool. I had been to one of their meetings and I was so jealous so when she came back I was excited to hear all about the trip. But she told me she couldn't tell me anything until she was reporting in class because that would ruin the surprise.

So she was called up to the front of the class by our Civics teacher who really is a nice guy and meant well, but didn't understand the consequences of what he said. When Pam started to give her report he asked her to tell us who funded her trip. "National Organization of Women," she said, and continued with her report. The teacher stopped her again and asked, "who else helped you with the funding?" She looked at him, paused and then said "The Gay and Lesbian Alliance" or whatever "Out Front Minnesota" was called then.

I was surprised. The rest of the class was surprised. And all of the guys in the class turned around and looked at me. I was worried they all thought I was gay too. And of course, being a teenage girl and a huge flirt, I did not want the boys to think I was gay.

I was never exactly mean to her, but I quit hanging out with her. And I know she knows why. I talked to my mom about it. My mom is pretty cool. She basically told me I needed to do what I felt was right for me at the time. I spent the rest of the school year, which was just a couple of months, feeling very bad about not hanging out with her anymore. About avoiding her simply so I wouldn't lose the attention of the guys.

We graduated in June of 1976. I'm not sure if she came to the ceremony or not.

In years after I was so ashamed of myself. I came to realize that was no way to treat another human being. And if guys were that stupid, they weren't for me anyway.

I could not for the life of me remember her last name and I spent years trying to figure out who she was so that I could apologize to her. This was really the only regret I had in my life for anything that I had done. It really bugged me. What bugged me most was how she must have felt.

Fast forward to about 1990. I was very active on a computer bulletin board called Top City. We were a community, or several communities, depending on how you look at it. The founder intended for Top City to be a place where everybody could hang out regardless of being gay or straight or trans or bi. I was in the forefront of explaining things to people who didn't want to hang out with straights or didn't want to hang out with gays. In fact I finessed the integration of trans women into the women's room on top City. It was a learning experience for all.

As the leader of the women's room, I set up monthly coffee get-togethers in different parts of the metro area. One very blustery snowy winter Sunday we had a coffee get together near my house so I posted that I would be there and anybody who could come should come but not to come if it was going to be too dangerous for driving. By the time we all got together it was very sunny, but there were many inches of new snow. I was sitting at a big round table by the window as Top City women showed up. There were maybe eight of us total when everyone was there that day. We introduced ourselves. On Top City we used handles but those who chose to also told us their real name. One of the women was named Pam. She was there with her girlfriend

Later on, as we were discussing various topics of current interest, we started talking about high school reunions. As I was on my high school reunion committee, I suggested that anybody who felt they had been overlooked by the reunion committees should contact the school they went to and find out who the contact person was for that class.

This woman named Pam mentioned that nobody in her class would be interested in seeing her anyway. When I asked her what school she went to, she told me Washburn. I opened my mouth to say something and I realized she was my age and therefore probably graduated in my class. So I verified this with her. As I was saying I didn't have her on my list of graduates, a light bulb went off in my head. And at the same time Pam said "Sheila?" and I said "Pam?" We jumped up, ran around the table and hugged each other, much to the astonishment of the other women.

It turned out this person I had been talking to for over a year was the person I had been wishing I could apologize to. I apologized then for my rude, hurtful treatment of her back in high school. She said there was no need to apologize, that she had put me in a difficult position. We talked and cried.

We kept in touch for several years.

At some point she told me she believed she was a man. We talked through the realities of getting some counseling to make sure she was ready to make the transition, and how to protect herself mentally for the other side. Depression is a reality.

At first her long-time girlfriend was onboard. But ultimately she could not deal with the changes and broke up. Pam and I lost track of each other and I often wondered if she completed the changes.

Fast forward to about 2000.

I was an attorney in north Minneapolis representing people sometimes two or more hours west of the cities. I would agree to meet them about halfway, usually in Chaska at Hardee's on Yellow Brick Road.

One day when I was meeting with a series of several separate clients, the manager came over to say he wanted to talk to me before I left. After my last client left, he sat down in the booth across from me. I thought he was going to tell me I couldn't meet with clients there anymore, but he asked if he looked familiar to me. I thought maybe he was a client or somehow I had met him out dancing or something. He was laughing. Finally he said he had gone to Washburn with me. Being part of the reunion committee I had studied every photo in the yearbook, but could not place this guy's face. Then he leaned across and in a quiet voice said "I am Pam Olson"

I was very surprised and made him stand up and turn around so I could see what the new body was all about. It was far from obvious that he had ever been a woman. He looked rugged. He looked good.

He asked me not to tell anyone because no one in his new life knew. He said he was happy, had a girlfriend and a cat, and was doing well at the job.

We kept in touch from time to time to check in. Maybe a couple times a year.

I was actually just about to call him to check in and grab a meal when I found out about the accident and his passing. I was very sad, but so glad he had found a better life, had tons of good friends and was loving life.

I knew he was sick. And I know he would not have wanted to become dependent on others.

I am blessed to be his friend and that he trusted me to share some of his feelings and transitions.

On the day of his memorial I left work early and went to the bar but couldn't make myself enter. I was concerned I might reveal Nick's secret.

I could not go in. I watched as many people entered for the memorial. And I stayed crying until people were leaving.

Sheila A. Scott
(set free to tell her story after reading
Nick's sister's eulogy)

The waters receive Nick's ashes
Photo courtesy of Nicks' sister, Cassandra Thurman

About the Author

Nick Spooner showed early signs of talent but rarely had time to write given his daytime – actually mostly nighttime – work as a private limo driver. Tragically his opportunity came when he was diagnosed with a terminal brain cancer. In his subsequent Facebook entries he revealed not only his talent, but his striking strengths of character.

About the Editor

Mona Gustafson Affinito, PhD., can be found at her website www.forgivenessoptions.com, and her blog at www.monagustafsonaffinito.com. She is the author of several books, including *When to Forgive*, *Forgiving One Page at a Time*, *Figs and Pomegranates and Special Cheeses* (the fictional story of the wife of Biblical Job) and *My Father's House* (published under her family name, Mona Gustafson.)

CPSIA information can be obtained
at www.ICGtesting.com
Printed in the USA
LVHW090737140721
692483LV00016B/836